Successful Problem-Solving for High-Functioning Students With Autism Spectrum Disorders

D1604973

Successful Problem-Solving for High-Functioning Students With Autism Spectrum Disorders

Kerry Mataya, MSEd, and Penney Owens, MEd, BCBA

Foreword by Brenda Smith Myles, PhD

Evidence-Based Strategy – Antecedent-Based Intervention

PUBLISHING

P.O. Box 23173
Shawnee Mission, Kansas 66283-0173
www.aapcpublishing.net

©2013 AAPC Publishing
P.O. Box 23173
Shawnee Mission, Kansas 66283-0173
www.aapcpublishing.net

Publisher's Cataloging-in-Publication

Mataya, Kerry.

   Successful problem-solving for high-functioning students with autism spectrum disorders : evidence-based strategy - antecedent-based intervention / Kerry Mataya, and Penney Owens. -- Shawnee Mission, Kan. : AAPC Publishing, c2013.

      p. ; cm.

      ISBN: 978-1-937473-21-1
      LCCN: 2012951821
      Includes bibliographical references.
      Summary: A tool for helping individuals with autism and similar disorders solve problems more effectively.--Publisher.

      1. Autism spectrum disorders--Treatment. 2. Problem solving in children. 3. Problem solving in adolescence. 4. Children with autism spectrum disorders--Treatment.
5. Problem-solving therapy. 6. Evidence-based psychotherapy. I. Owens, Penney. II. Title.

RJ506.A9 M38 2012
618.92/85882--dc23   1212

This book is designed in Palatino and Helvetica Neue.

Printed in the United States of America.

FOREWORD

I am a life-long learner. Each day I learn new pieces of information – some important, others fascinating, and a small number trivial. For example, if you drop your cellphone in water, it is best not to try to power it on while it is still wet. If you are interested in understanding the relationship between music and math, you can study Bach. And if you run out of toothpaste, baking powder is a good replacement.

Underlying most of these life lessons, as well as many others, is the ability to problem solve. In fact, from one perspective, we can view our lives as a series of problems that we must solve. I don't think this is a pessimistic view of life, but rather an acceptance of the many challenges that come our way daily.

We start our day with problems. You get up in the morning planning to wear a certain shirt, but it is not in the closet. You find another shirt. You go to put on a specific pair of shoes, but can only find the left one. So you search until you find the matching shoe under your bed. You head to the kitchen for a quick breakfast; oatmeal sounds good. But there is no oatmeal. You settle for a granola bar. As you are leaving your house, you reach for your keys. They are always on the hook by the door leading to the garage, but this morning they are not. Somehow they have ended up on the bathroom counter. When you arrive at work, a colleague asks about your morning. You reply that it was ordinary – *and that is because you were able to quickly and automatically solve each problem you encountered.*

Many individuals, including many with autism spectrum disorders (ASD), do not seem to inherently have problem-solving skills and, as a result, struggle with the everyday activities of life – finding a comb, deciding what to do on the weekend, planning how to afford that new television that seems out of reach on your budget, and so forth. The lack of problem-solving skills or having inefficient problem-solving skills affects your quality of life and can act as barriers to developing relationships, completing tasks, seeking help when needed, and getting and keeping a job.

Kerry Mataya and Penney Owens, recognizing the complexity of life's problems and the challenges that learners on the spectrum experience in this area, have created a problem-solving rubric and curriculum that I can only refer to as brilliant! It is elegant in its simplicity and rich in its breadth and depth. It is applicable to young and old alike and is easily generalized to most situations.

Several years ago, I learned that Kerry Mataya was a genius, and when she partners with people, such as Penney Owens, it is likely that her partners are gifted also. Kerry and Penney have used this model successfully with the myriad learners on the spectrum whom they have supported in home, school, and community settings. This common sense approach – an evidence-based antecedent-based intervention – teaches problem-solving in a manner that supports learners with ASD to reach their limitless potential.

Brenda Smith Myles, PhD

TABLE OF CONTENTS

INTRODUCTION

The last 10 minutes of the boys' social skills group for 10- to 12-year-olds is always devoted to unstructured activities. The boys are encouraged to do something with a peer, but they can play alone, if they wish. Raj elected to play a game on the iPad he had tucked into his backpack. One of the newest boys in the group, Luke, was sitting alone and was obviously unhappy.

As I sat with him and listened as Luke described how unfair it was that Raj was playing on an electronic device and he was not, I knew we needed to discuss a better way to problem solve. Instead of letting the problem go or talking it out with me, he continued to perseverate on the problem rather than focusing on a solution. In his mind, there was no room for resolution.

As an autism consultant, I have worked with students in a variety of settings and situations – from after-school social skills groups, life skills planning, and IEP preparation and participation, to summer drama, sports, and overnight camps. Regardless of the setting, problem-solving is a persistent challenge among students with autism spectrum disorders (ASD), even those who are otherwise high functioning.

Problem-solving is fundamental to effective communication and social interaction; therefore, strengthening these skills will increase success in community activities, long-term relationships, employment, and overall independent living.

Research has shown that individuals with ASD have deficits in planning, abstract problem-solving, and multitasking (Hill, 2004). Moreover, they have difficulty applying knowledge and skills across settings and integrating learned material into real life. That is, although they may be able to memorize facts and information, they often do not recall and apply the information when needed (Collucci, 2011; Moore, 2002; Myles & Southwick, 2005).

To further complicate their issues related to the ability to problem solve using abstract reasoning, individuals with ASD have difficulty identifying and forming concepts (Minshew, Meyer, & Goldstein, 2002). Temple Grandin (1999), a well-known author with ASD, explains how, in order to form concepts, she sorts pictures into categories similar to computer files. To form the concept of orange, for example, she sees many different orange objects, such as oranges, pumpkins, orange juice, and marmalade.

There is an abundance of resources in the area of social skills for individuals with ASD, but significantly fewer address problem-solving. I developed the Problem-Solving Chart to help fill this void. The Problem-Solving Chart teaches how to effectively communicate and interact with others. The strategy has worked in my practice for several years with many individuals with high-functioning ASD, from kindergarten through adulthood. In addition, many teachers and therapists have utilized the chart in their schools and social groups with positive results.

Teachers and parents who have used the Problem-Solving Chart in classrooms and homes have reported an increase in students' self-advocacy skills. Additionally, when students have been successful in talking out a problem, they are more likely to repeat the strategy in other situations – and are likely to gain self-confidence with each successful exchange. When they finally learn to "let it go and move on" – an important life skill for everyone – their lives are changed. They no longer have to hold on to negative feelings for months and years, often leading to frustration, anger, and even suicide.

How This Book Can Help

The objective of this book is to teach you how to integrate the Problem-Solving Chart into classrooms, homes, and social skills groups to help individuals with ASD to learn to problem solve effectively. The strategy is considered an evidence-based strategy (EBP) under the category of *antecedent-based interventions* (Centers for Medicare and Medicaid Services, 2009; National Autism Center, 2009; National Professional Development Center on Autism Spectrum Disorders, n.d.). That is, it is designed to be put in place prior to a behavior to prevent its occurrence. In addition, it has social validity. Problem-solving is a skill that is used across the lifespan in all environments.

I hope you find the Problem-Solving Chart to be helpful. While the challenges of teaching problem-solving may seem daunting, the barriers can be overcome. You may not see changes overnight, but keep at it. Through repetition of vocabulary and a simple protocol for problem-solving, you will succeed and, best of all, the child or student will benefit immensely now and in the future.

Best of luck,

Kerry Mataya

NOTE: Reproducing and laminating the chart (see p. 54) and using a dry-erase marker allows you to use the chart multiple times.

CHAPTER ONE

What Is the Problem-Solving Chart?

Many individuals with autism spectrum disorders (ASD) have difficulty coming up with effective ways to solve problems.

TJ, a high school student who has ASD, was assigned the role of leader for a small-group activity. TJ planned the group project and assigned tasks. She was not pleased with the work of the other team members; nonetheless, the team received an A on the project.

The teacher later complimented TJ on her success as a team leader and asked her what strategies she had used to help the team to produce such good work. TJ responded, "Thank you. It was easy. I just told the team that they were lazy and stupid, and I fired them. Then I did the project the right way myself."

Going through life followed by a trail of unresolved difficulties can make every day and every experience a challenge. The list on page 4 shows behaviors that may indicate somebody does not have the necessary problem-solving skills.

Common Indicators of Deficits in Problem-Solving Skills

- Being bothered by a problem for extended periods of time
- Lashing out at others
- Remembering an unresolved problem for years and bringing it up often
- Experiencing a cycle of negative thoughts
- Difficulty maintaining positive interactions
- Unable to broaden focus to include all relevant facts
- Unable to identify relevant parts of problem situations
- Focusing on some aspect of a situation to the exclusion of all else
- Attaching extreme emotional connotations to seemingly minor events
- Difficulty asking for help
- Unwillingness to listen to other persons' problems and concerns
- Difficulty expressing opinions using neutral tone and body language
- Difficulty losing in game situation
- Unwillingness to try potential strategies that may resolve the problem

The following describes the case of Davis, a fourth grader, who needed assistance with problem-solving skills. Davis has a diagnosis of high-functioning ASD.

Davis was usually able to complete his homework assignments within 30 minutes and with very little "drama." One evening while doing homework at the kitchen table, Davis hesitated on each step of his assignments. He argued with his mother about the instructions and announced that his homework was "not fair." He became increasingly upset and began to cry and yell. In the middle of his homework crisis, he screamed, "It is going to storm tomorrow!"

This apparently unrelated outburst made his mother realize that Davis was distressed by the forecast of a severe storm and that, as a result, even a routine homework assignment had become overwhelming to him. Davis was not able to sort through the challenges that he was facing. He had not told her about his fear, nor had he sought reassurance.

As is true with many with ASD, Davis needed a strategy for problem-solving – to help him recognize problems, identify a solution, and move on.

Much has been written about the characteristics of autism – deficits in theory of mind, emotional recognition, and executive functioning – that may underlie the social challenges experienced by individuals with ASD. That is, a combination of executive functioning deficits, including difficulties with organization, cognitive flexibility, inhibition, prioritizing, multitasking, monitoring, and planning (Abendroth & Damico, 2009; Crane, Pring, Ryder, & Hermelin, 2011; Hill, 2004; Hill & Bird, 2006; Geurts, Verté, Oosterlaan, Roéyers, & Sergeant, 2004; Ostryn & Wolfe, 2011). With these difficulties in understanding their social world along with deficits in executive functioning, it is not surprising that social conflicts are particularly difficult for individuals on the autism spectrum to solve.

The Problem-Solving Chart is an instructional tool that helps address these underlying deficits. The chart provides a concrete structure for the process of problem-solving based on the premise that it is important to see the "big picture" of the situation and identify specific courses of action that may be taken to solve it. Due to their rigid thinking, tendency toward obsessive thought, and low frustration tolerance (Frith, 2004; Kim, Szatmari, Bryson, Streiner, & Wilson, 2000), individuals with ASD often get stuck focusing on the problem itself and not on a solution.

In order to develop a strategy for teaching how to problem-solve, it is first necessary to review the problem-solving process. Steps to problem-solving generally include the following:

1. **Identify the problem**
2. **Determine possible solutions**
3. **Identify consequences**
4. **Develop a plan of action with the most appropriate choice**
5. **Evaluate your choice**

It is important that individuals with ASD learn to visualize the whole problem-solving structure in order to make a decision that works for a given situation. The word "visualize" is significant here. Most people with ASD process information more effectively when it is presented in a visual rather than an auditory manner. The Problem-Solving Chart is a visual support that facilitates understanding of the whole problem-solving structure – the problem and the possible solutions. When using the chart, if possible, color the three positive and most effective options (Seek Help From Adult, Talk It Out and Compromise, and Let It Go and Move On) blue and color the fourth (Let It Bother You) red.

Basic Problem-Solving Chart

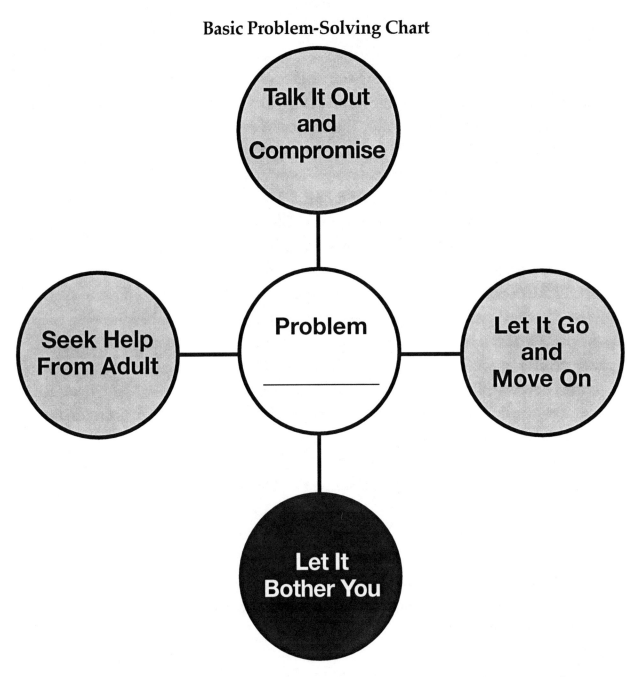

Since what is considered an appropriate response will vary with each situation, the Problem-Solving Chart is set up as a choice board, and the strategies that make up the process are not designed to be used in a particular order. However, while learning to use the chart, many students* start at Seek Help From Adult and then rotate clockwise through the other strategies: Talk It Out and Compromise, Let It Go and Move On, and Let It Bother You.

---

*While the Problem-Solving Chart may be used across a wide age range, including adulthood, throughout this book we use the term *student* to denote the person who is learning this problem-solving method. Also, we alternate between the pronouns "he" and "she" when referring to individual students.

Let's look at each strategy.

Seek Help From Adult

A trusted adult can offer a different perspective on the situation, and perhaps even a solution to the problem. Another person's perspective can be helpful for anyone who is stuck in a situation. Seeking help is a particularly important strategy, especially for young students, until they are able to independently Talk It Out and Compromise or Let It Go and Move On.

Talk It Out and Compromise

If the problem involves another person, talking it out can help both parties feel they are being heard and understood. A compromise can turn a problem into a win-win situation for both parties.

Let It Go and Move On

There are many times in life when things don't go our way and the only acceptable solution is to let it go and move on. This is a life skill that everyone needs to learn, and it is often a helpful solution if other strategies have been tried without resolution, or if the problem involves something that cannot be changed.

Let It Bother You

It is common for a student with high-functioning ASD to get stuck on a problem long after others have moved on (Ritvo et al., 2008). This is not an acceptable long-term solution because it creates distress for the student and does not allow him to focus on other things. The option to Let It Bother You is included on the chart to help the student to understand that being stuck is a choice but that he can select – and is strongly encouraged to – from more productive alternatives.

In the next chapter, we will look at how to put the Problem-Solving Chart into practice.

CHAPTER TWO

How to Use the Problem-Solving Chart

Teaching a student to independently use the Problem-Solving Chart and to generalize problem-solving skills requires individualization and patience. Since the Problem-Solving Chart is likely to involve a new set of vocabulary terms and concepts, it is generally introduced and taught in either one-to-one or small-group settings. Once the student understands the terms and concepts, the chart may be used for teaching problem-solving skills to a group. It is also possible to use the chart with a student during a group activity without him becoming the focus of the group's attention by nonverbally prompting (using a predetermined sign, such as pointing to the chart) the student to use the chart if she is having trouble with problem-solving.

Preteach each area of the Problem-Solving Chart in a low-stress situation. When initially teaching this strategy, spend approximately 15-20 minutes reviewing the terminology; that is, go through the problem-solving steps outlined in Chapter One and explain the names for the specific parts of the chart. Then, using hypothetical, as well as actual, situations that have had frustrating consequences in the student's life, describe in some detail how each problem was handled. Next, determine how the problem could have been handled differently for better results. Typical situations addressed include misplacing something, being last in line, not finding a partner for an activity, learning that a friend lied, being falsely accused of something, getting in trouble at school, etc.

Once the strategy has been pretaught, it is time to put it into action as problems occur in daily life. The time required to work through a problem will vary with each student and with each situation. Typically, working through the chart the first few times takes approximately 20-30 minutes. This will allow you to teach the student the flow of considering each possible solution to determine its potential effectiveness. Once students have become familiar with the terminology and have consistently reached a successful solution in at least three to five consecutive situations, the process will take less time. For "experienced" students, it typically takes 2-3 seconds to determine an effective solution from the chart.

General Problem-Solving Steps

The following steps will make the problem-solving process run more smoothly:

Determine the problem

Assess the strategies/review options

Solve the problem

Follow up

> **NOTE: Review the whole chart in one setting and make sure the chart is available for visual reference in every problem-solving situation.**

Step 1. Determine the Problem – Describe the Problem Situation

Begin with the middle circle (Problem) (see p. 11) by asking, "What is the problem?" Listen carefully as the student describes the situation (if he is able). Using only a few words, write in the problem circle the main idea of what the student said so you can refer to it. **If it is not written down, the original problem may turn into another problem ... and then another.** Remember to include a picture or drawing for students who are poor readers or unable to read, or for those who learn best with additional visual cues – see page 11.

Confirm with the student that the problem has been correctly identified. *Do not move on to the next step until you and the student have a mutual understanding of the problem.* Students with high-functioning ASD may get hung up on wording and be unable to move on until the situation is worded correctly. If the student offers a slight wording change that is appropriate to the situation, make it.

> Some students are unaware of the problem and, therefore, do not realize a need for problem-solving. In these situations, someone (e.g., a peer, a teacher, a family member, or a friend) must identify the problem to help the student recognize it. Once the problem has been determined, the student can work through the remaining problem-solving strategies (moving on to Step 2).

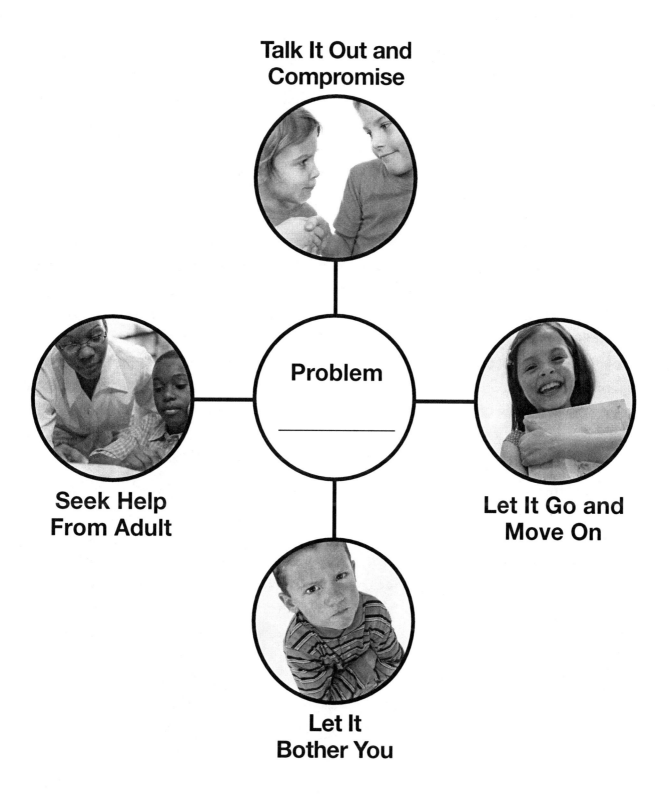

**Talk It Out and
Compromise**

Problem
_____

**Seek Help
From Adult**

**Let It Go and
Move On**

**Let It
Bother You**

Step 2. Assess the Strategies – Review the Options

Begin this step by asking the student what he did when the problem occurred. For example, a student might respond that she yelled at someone, cried, or kicked another child as a response to the problem.

Remind the student that there are only three effective strategies on the chart to solve the problem – Seek Help From an Adult; Talk It Out and Compromise; and Let It Go and Move On. Carefully review the three choices aloud and apply them to the problem to determine several possible solutions. Ask if the student has tried one of the three choices to resolve the situation. Help him to see how each strategy can yield a positive result. Explain that Let It Bother You is not a desired solution. Trying out and assessing the three preferential strategies helps students to see the benefits of the alternatives to Let It Bother You.

Students with high-functioning ASD are not likely to find every option equally acceptable. One of the options (e.g., compromising) may be particularly difficult for a given student, who, as a result, prefers to talk to an adult. This is one of the beauties of this method as there are several acceptable options to choose from when having to solve a problem. It is important to remember that a student must be willing and able to use each strategy if applicable to the situation.

Getting in the Right Frame of Mind to Problem Solve

Some students will need a break to cool down and lower their stress level before beginning the problem-solving process. Because this step is not needed by all students, it is not included in the actual Problem-Solving Chart. The illustration of Controlling Behavior on page 36 shows how the additional strategy of a break was incorporated into the Problem-Solving Chart for a particular student. It is not appropriate to begin the Problem-Solving Chart when a student is exhibiting signs of rumbling or rage. Rumbling is the first stage of the rage cycle, and includes behaviors that can accelerate toward rage (Myles & Southwick, 2005). The time that it takes to return to low stress will vary with each student.

Myles and Southwick outlined several ways to assist a student in returning to a state of lower stress, including home base, redirecting, antiseptic bouncing, and just walk and don't talk.

Home base is a physical place where a person can go to escape the overstimulation of the environment.

Redirecting means providing an alternative focus of attention in order to help to diminish the stress.

Antiseptic bouncing involves removing the student from an anxiety-charged environment by creating a situation in which he can calm down.

Just walk and don't talk means minimizing the use of words to allow the emotionally provoked student to be able to become calm.

The Incredible 5-Point Scale (Buron & Curtis, 2012) is also a great resource to use for understanding and controlling behavior. "1" on this scale is the least or mildest form of the behavior or attribute that is being measured or explained. The intensity increases or intensifies as the scale progresses from "1" to "5." This allows many behaviors or attributes to be compared and to be explained by identifying them in relationship to one another on this 5-point scale, providing an easier way to understand the continuum.

From *The Incredible 5-Point Scale: The Significantly Improved and Expanded Second Edition* by Kari Dunn Buron and Mitzi Curtis. AAPC Publishing © 2012.; www.aapcpublishing.net. Used with permission.

When the student is asked to consider a solution (e.g., "Would Talking It Out and Compromising be a good option?"), she may respond with "no" or "I don't know." If she answers "no," try to rephrase the question so that she has to use more than just "yes" or" no" answers (i.e., use open-ended questions such as "What would Bobby do if you offered to play his game first and your game second?").

Using prompt questions to help students to infer mental states can increase appropriate choices (Kaland, Mortensen, & Smith, 2011). Prompts to maneuver through the Problem-Solving Chart will vary, depending on the student's age and ability.

In the following, prompts are separated into two categories, beginner and advanced. *Beginner prompts* are used for students who need ample guidance when going through the chart. *Advanced prompts* are used for students who do not require as much guidance determining the problem but may need support to think of alternate solutions.

Sample Prompts for Reviewing Options	
Beginner Prompts	**Advanced Prompts**
Beginner Prompts to Determine the Problem Okay, let's go through this. • How do you feel right now? • It looks like you feel ___. • You have a problem. • Let's talk about the problem. (This assumes you have to help the student figure it out.) • Let's see what you could do.	**Advanced Prompts to Determine the Problem** • What is the problem? • Is that your only problem? • Is that your main problem?
Beginner Prompts to Discover Solutions *Seek Help* • Could you ask someone for help? • What could you do if an adult was not around? • If you did try seeking help, what happened? • How can you seek help differently? • If you did not seek help, let's talk about what might happen if you did seek help.	**Advanced Prompts to Discover Solutions** *Seek Help* • Have you tried to get help from an adult or someone you trust? • Why not? (If the answer to the first prompt is "no") • Did they help you? Do you think that they could help you? • Could you have done something differently so that this might have worked out better? • Let's think about this strategy. Could you try it? What would you do if you tried it?
Beginner Prompts to *Talk It Out and Compromise* • Could you Talk It Out and Compromise? • If you did try talking it out, what happened? • What did you say to talk it out? • How did you say it? (role-play use of words and tone of voice) • How could you talk it out differently? • If you did not talk it out, let's talk about what might happen if you did talk it out. • What did you say to try to compromise? • Let's practice compromising. (Role-play use of scripts ✔ to lead to a compromise)	**Advanced Prompts to *Talk It Out and Compromise*** • Have you tried to talk it out? • Why not? • What happened when you tried to Talk It Out and Compromise? • Why do you think it did not work? • Could you have done it differently so this might have worked better? • Let's think about this strategy. Could you try it? What would you do if you tried it?
Beginner Prompts to *Let It Go and Move On* • Could you let it go and move on? • Why not? • Let's talk about what might happen if you did let it go.	**Advanced Prompts to *Let It Go and Move On*** • Have you tried to let it go and move on? • Why is it difficult to let it go? • Can you change the situation by continuing to dwell on it? • If you are still talking about the problem, you have not yet moved on. • What is something you can try that might help you to let it go and move on. (Refer to pages 48-49 for strategies for letting it go.)
Beginner Prompts to *Let It Bother You* • You are still letting it bother you. • Do you want to keep feeling this way? • Is this fun? • Do you feel like the problem is solved?	**Advanced Prompts to *Let It Bother You*** • Is letting it continue to bother you what you really want? • Do you want to go back and revisit the other solutions?

TEACHER TIP

Scripting

Defined as providing specific mental or verbal scripts of what to think or say (Wichnick, Vener, Pyrtek, & Poulson, 2010), scripting can be very helpful for students who focus on the problem rather than the solution. Use written scripts of what to think or say in problem situations (e.g., "Oh well, no big deal." or "I'll try it!").

Lydia had a hard time trying a peer's suggestion if it was something that she did not want to do. This made it difficult for her to work in groups, and peers felt she was being selfish.

Although Lydia used the Problem-Solving Chart, she often let problems bother her until the other children gave in and ended up going with her idea. She was successful with the Talking It Out and Compromise strategy, but her teacher felt like she tried to negotiate everything. She wanted Lydia to "go with the flow" more when the whole group wanted to do something else. Her teacher paired scripting with the Problem-Solving Chart to assist Lydia in letting go of her concerns and participating with her peers. Her script was "I'll try it." This script was appropriate for Lydia both to think in her head and say aloud. At first, she received priming of the script with additional praise for using the script appropriately until she was able to use it independently. This phrase was very successful for Lydia, and something she continues to use.

Scripting can be an excellent tool for helping a student to achieve independence in using the problem-solving strategies more quickly.

Step 3. Solve the Problem – Make a Choice and Carry It Out

Once the student has assessed the strategies on the Problem-Solving Chart in Step 2, it is time for him to choose the most appropriate strategy to solve the problem at hand. This step, Step 3, consists of following through with the strategy chosen from the chart. The benefit here is that students will receive natural positive reinforcement (✔) when the solution they choose yields successful results.

Leon often had difficulty during group projects because he wanted to force his ideas upon others without a consensus. Other students did not want to be in Leon's group because of his harsh and condescending tone.

Mrs. Spurlock worked with Leon on talking it out with his group using a neutral tone and trying to find a compromise. Leon was surprised to see how effective this was for him. He began to choose the strategy of Talking It Out and Compromising more frequently because of the great results he achieved.

As a result, the other students began to choose Leon to be in their groups and seemed to enjoy his contributions. For the first time, Leon began to think of some of his peers as friends.

TEACHER TIP

Natural vs. External Reinforcement

Natural reinforcement. Natural reinforcement includes reinforcers within the situation itself (Nefdt, Koegel, Singer, & Gerber, 2009). Although reinforcement can be effective when it happens in natural settings without planning, you might have to point it out to a student with ASD when it happens.

While Ashton had developed many social skills, he did not entirely grasp the concept of cause and effect. One day, after a successful recess, his teacher pointed out how cause and effect and natural reinforcement impacted him. She said, "Who did you play with at recess? You had fun. By letting the problem go and moving on, you had a great time." She also encouraged him to let things go in the future so that he could continue to have fun with his friends at the playground.

Think of this almost as providing proof to the student that something worked. The student may not notice or may forget, so always point it out.

External reinforcement. Reinforcement for positive behavior is used to increase the likelihood of the behavior happening again. If natural reinforcers are absent or

---

are not strong enough or rapid enough, it is essential to provide additional reinforcement when the student demonstrates positive problem-solving behaviors (Vismara & Rogers, 2010). External reinforcement has to be meaningful for the student. External reinforcement may have to be changed over time in order to maintain momentum toward acquiring a new skill or behavior; however, this type of reinforcement should be faded so that the individual can focus on doing the skill independently without the external need for reinforcement.

Luis was doing well with Letting Things Go and Moving On when it came to most things. He used the script of "oh well, no big deal," which helped him tremendously.

Nevertheless, his parents noticed that he had difficulty letting things go when it came to physical problems (e.g., getting hit with a basketball, accidentally banging his leg coming down a slide). Luis had a very low tolerance for getting hurt and seemed to use physical pain and problems as an excuse to get out of problem situations (e.g., "My back is really sore, so I can't do it"). His parents used external reinforcement of money to help him to learn the strategy of letting go with regard to physical pain. To reinforce this skill, Luis earned $1.00 for each time his parents caught him letting something go. He earned double reinforcement of $2.00 for each instance of letting go of a problem that was physical. The motivation of the monetary reinforcement helped to change his behavior in only two weeks.

Step 4. Follow Up

Once the student has solved the problem, set a plan for follow-up. Follow-up should address how the student will handle similar situations in the future. Discuss which strategies were effective and which were not effective and why. Reviewing the Problem-Solving Chart typically leads to faster results and increased independence in choosing an effective problem-solving strategy next time.

Moving Through the Strategies Toward a Solution

As mentioned, often students with high-functioning ASD are unaware of the problem until someone points it out to them. But even after someone has specifically stated that there is a problem, it is important for many learners to define the problem and work through the problem-solving strategies. Although there is no particular sequence to maneuvering around the Problem-Solving Chart, the typical sequence is to begin with Seek Help and then rotate through the strategies clockwise. We will now take a look at how the process plays out.

Seek Help From an Adult

Seeking help from an adult is usually an easy strategy and, therefore, used quite often. The security of being able to take problems to somebody else and have that person help work out a solution is generally easier than other problem-solving choices. If you are working with a student who is shy or has poor social skills, he may need to learn how to seek help from an adult using a predetermined script (e.g., a note card that reads "I need your help") or a visual support (e.g., picture symbol of a child talking to a teacher; a red/green card the student can flip to the red side when he or she needs help).

The student may also need to be directly taught to seek help from an adult in a private setting in order to avoid tattling or blurting out his thoughts in front of others. If this is the case, avoid teaching just a rule, such as "Wait until the teacher is alone to discuss the problem" or "Ask to discuss the problem privately." Instead, teach the student WHY it is best to discuss the problem in private.

Also, consider teaching concepts that may seem obvious to others but may not be apparent to the student with ASD (the hidden curriculum). These concepts include the following:

- Some infractions are minor and do not require immediate attention or consequences.
- Peers may get angry at you if you tell on them, even if you are right about what they did.
- It may be difficult for others to concentrate on their work if you are talking loudly in the same room.

Demonstrate effective ways to seek help by using visual supports such as cartooning or a written list of the steps for seeking help from an adult. Video modeling is another effective strategy (Deitchman, Reeve, Reeve, & Progar, 2010).

Sample Written List of Steps for Seeking Help From an Adult

Getting the Teacher's Attention	
	Wait for the teacher to finish speaking.
	Raise your hand without waving.
	Get attention by using the expression, "Excuse me."
	Wait for the teacher to call on you.

From Lofland, K. (2010). *Getting the teacher's attention.* Unpublished manuscript. Bloomington, IN: Indiana Resource Center on Autism. Used with permission.

✓ TEACHER TIP

Video Modeling

The use of video can be a valuable tool for teaching a student how to apply problem-solving strategies (cf., Bellini & Peters, 2008). This is typically done by videotaping a student working through the problem-solving process in real time within his natural environment and later reviewing the video footage with the student.

> NOTE: It is important to videotape the student modeling or applying appropriate problem-solving strategies rather than videotaping the student letting a problem bother him. Some students have negative or adverse reactions to seeing their negative behvior on video and might feel the adult is trying to embarass or shame them.

Liam was playing flag football with his friends. He has a negative history with one of the students on the other team. If that student pulls his flag or tries to block him, Liam typically views the interaction as unfair and overly negative.

Liam was prepared to be videotaped during his flag football game and was reminded to choose an effective problem-solving strategy rather than letting it bother him. During play, a group leader videotaped Liam's interaction with the particular peer during a play where the ball was fumbled and the two boys both went to recover it. Liam's glasses were knocked off during the recovery, and the other student went away with the ball. Liam's response was initially frustration, but he quickly brushed himself off and put his glasses back on to get back in the game for the next play.

This videotape was shown to Liam as a positive example of how he applied the technique of Letting It Go and Moving On quickly. The outcome was that he was able to continue to have fun in the game.

As students get older, continuously seeking help from another person is not an appropriate long-term solution. Students who seek help from adults in every problem situation must be taught the additional strategies on the Problem-Solving Chart. Consider which skills are age-appropriate. If a student continues to seek help to solve problems that her peers are most often able to solve independently, it is time to encourage her to try other strategies. Keep in mind that the student has experienced success with problem-solving by seeking help. This success is reinforcing (natural reinforcer); therefore, students may need to be offered reinforcement (external reinforcer) for practicing other strategies.

Austin was a first-grade student with ASD. Austin's peers perceived him as a tattler. If students were talking when they were supposed to be quiet, he would loudly tell on them. Many classmates thought of him as the "rule police."

Austin needed to learn to hold his thoughts until he could talk to the teacher privately without the other children knowing that he was tattling. He also needed to know specific reasons for seeking help or not seeking help. Although he quickly sought help from an adult, Austin did not do so in the correct manner. Austin's special education teacher created rules so he would know when to seek help from the teacher (i.e., emergencies, concerns for safety) and when to keep it to himself. She also taught him what his peers thought when they heard him "tattling." By the end of the school year, Seeking Help From an Adult was often a successful strategy for Austin – because it was age appropriate and provided the solutions and support he needed.

Talk It Out and Compromise

This strategy requires all involved to talk and listen. A student with ASD is likely to see the situation from only one perspective: his own. However, compromise is a necessary component of this step. After both people (all parties) verbalize their concerns, they have to come up with a resolution by using one of the Three Rules of Compromise. Although there are many ways to compromise, we chose the following rules because they are appropriate to use into adulthood.

Three Rules of Compromise

■ **Majority vote** – The conflict is settled by taking a vote. The majority prevails. For example, some of the students want to play baseball, some want to play video games. They take a vote. More students want to play baseball; therefore, using the majority vote rule, the solution to the problem is that everyone plays baseball.

■ **First _____ Then _____** – The conflict is settled by dividing the time and doing what each person wants for half of the time. For example, Juan wants to play video games. Pierre wants to play baseball. Using the First _____ Then_____ rule of compromise, they determine to play video games first and to play baseball second. Focus on putting the other person's idea first.

■ **Brainstorming** – The conflict is settled by putting two or more ideas together to form one solution. For example, Mike wants to play tag and other students want to play race cars. Mike suggests that the group play "race car tag," whereby they play the game of tag while acting like race cars.

Visual Support for Three Rules of Compromise

COMPROMISE

1 Majority Vote

2 First _____ Then _____

3 Brainstorm (put 2 ideas together)

Matt, a third grader with ASD, was in a social skills group and had learned the Three Rules of Compromise. He and his friends were trying to decide on a game to play, but he did not like the game the other kids suggested. So he asked, "Who wants to play cars?" Half of the group wanted to play cars, and the other half wanted to play something else. Matt tried to compromise by asking what the others wanted to play. Once he learned of their idea, Matt suggested that the group first do what the other half wanted to do and then play with cars. Everyone agreed.

Talking It Out and Compromising was a successful solution for Matt in this situation. Ideally, if the strategy had not worked, Matt would have continued to use his Problem-Solving Chart and worked through the available strategies (Seek Help From an Adult to determine what the group should play or Let It Go and play the game the group wants).

Let It Go and Move On

This strategy is often the most difficult for a student with ASD to learn. In fact, this is the main reason why the Problem-Solving Chart was developed in the first place. In a given situation, the student can attempt to Seek Help From an Adult, but that may not work because the adult may not be available at the time needed. Talking It Out and Compromising may not work either. Sometimes the answer is simply to Let It Go and Move On.

Letting It Go and Moving On requires a mental shift in focus from the problem to something not related to the problem. Consider the problem situation above in which

Matt wanted to play cars and others did not. If the group had not been able to reach a compromise, Matt could have chosen another preferred activity such as playing with Legos. He could enjoy this activity by himself or with others.

Antoine, a fifth grader, got upset when his classmates sat in "his" seat at lunch (there were no real "assigned" seats). Antoine contemplated Talking It Out, but previous experiences with his classmates had taught him that they would not talk about things and were unwilling to compromise. He told the teacher that someone was in his seat. His classmates saw that he was telling (Seeking Help From Adult) and later picked on him for tattling. Antoine was upset about this for an entire week. In the meantime, his classmates enjoyed watching him stay angry about the loss of that particular seat day after day. The longer he remained upset, the more negative attention he received.

We showed Antoine the Problem-Solving Chart and directly taught him how to Let It Go and Move On with regard to what had happened. The teacher took Antoine to the cafeteria when there were no other students present. She modeled a positive way to handle the situation. She taught him to say the script "It's okay to change seats sometimes. I will Let It Go and Move On" and sit in a different seat.

The teacher also wrote the script down and put it in Antoine's lunch box. She then reinforced (externally) Antoine for successfully practicing this strategy. After the third day of using the chart, Antoine was able to shift focus and sit by his new friends at the lunch table and talk about video games. His resistance to reacting to the boys who took "his" seat showed his ability to Let It Go and Move On. Although three days would appear to be a long time before seeing results from using the chart, Antoine was known for holding onto perceptions of others, often plotting revenge for months without letting go, so three days was a success! Antoine gained control and confidence when he was able to verbalize that he had truly moved on.

Let It Bother You

Students with ASD often have a hard time letting go and moving on, which results in things building up and bothering them. **This is not a good solution to a problem, because it can lead to decreased ability to maintain attention to other topics, as well as to increased anxiety and unhappiness.**

Letting It Bother You is defined as perseverating on a problem – being stuck without a real solution. It is evidenced by behaviors such as yelling, avoidance, crying, running away, and hitting. This type of perseveration may also be evidenced in the form of clenched teeth, frowning, narrowed eyebrows, a red face, and a racing heart.

Point out these physical signs to the student to facilitate self-understanding. Also, explain that if the student is still talking about the problem after 2-5 minutes, she is letting it bother her and needs to go back to the Problem-Solving Chart to work through another strategy.

When approaching a student who is letting a problem bother her, remember that the student may need more than 5 minutes to cool down before she is able to begin the problem-solving process. Refer to page 12 for cool-down strategies.

> *Coen was upset because William said that everyone at school was his friend. His youth group director, Ms. Gonzalez, took Coen aside and talked to him about Letting It Go and Moving On. Ms. Gonzalez made sure that Coen knew she would talk to William about it but that it would be embarrassing to William for her to bring it up in front of the youth group.*
>
> *But Coen would not let it go. He continued to let William's comment bother him and no longer wanted to participate in youth group because he claimed that he could not attend a group with someone who thought everyone was his friend. Coen knew that having everyone as a friend is not possible, and he was "stuck" on that. Because he could not problem-solve using other strategies, he missed out on a great opportunity to socialize with peers.*

Revisit this chapter as needed to review specifics on prompts and strategies to facilitate maximum success with students. For additional examples of how the Problem-Solving Chart may be implemented, see Chapter Four.

Mastery of these problem-solving strategies has the potential to change the course of somebody's life. The importance of these skills warrants keeping accurate records of the steps taken to teach the skills and the progress made toward mastery. Steps for data collection will be discussed in the following chapter.

CHAPTER THREE

Data Collection and Assessment

It is important to collect data regularly while using the Problem-Solving Chart, as it allows you to monitor your students' progress toward developing effective problem-solving skills. Additionally, for students who are receiving special education services, data collection is a legal requirement. Data help to determine if the individualized education program (IEP) has been faithfully followed, if a specific strategy is effective, and if goals and objectives are appropriate.

Objectives provide a preset goal or expectation for mastery. The IEP includes a statement of the current skill level that a student has reached and an agreed-upon expectation for mastery – the objective. Data are collected to determine if the objectives have been mastered.

Bekah has difficulty engaging in "free play" at school. Her peers have begun to avoid her at recess. When she is able to join an activity, she insists that her peers play the games by her rules.

Bekah inevitably ends up sitting on the bench at the side of the playground crying because she has no friends. This pattern of behavior has been going on for many months. This represents her current skill level, also known as her present level of performance.

The staff members recognize that Bekah is not ready to resolve these conflicts on her own. They state the following objective for Bekah: Using the Problem-Solving Chart, Bekah will select Seek Help From an Adult and successfully ask for help 4 out of 5 times (80%) that she experiences conflict with her peers during recess. Such data are collected on a data collection sheet. Below is a sample of objectives related to problem-solving.

Example of IEP Objectives

Note: To make goals measurable, remember to assign criteria for mastery (e.g., in 9 out of 10 opportunities or 90% of the time).

1. Student will demonstrate understanding of problem-solving strategies by verbalizing definitions and examples of problem-solving strategies: Seek Help From an Adult, Talk It Out and Compromise, Let It Go and Move On, and Let It Bother You.
2. Student will verbalize his understanding of at least five negative results associated with letting something bother you.
3. Student will Seek Help From Adult using verbal requests.
4. Student will Seek Help From Adult using nonverbal gestures to secure adult attention.
5. Student will Talk It Out and Compromise with peers in structured setting (e.g., group projects, classroom assignments).
6. Student will Talk It Out and Compromise with peers in unstructured setting (e.g., recess, lunch, hallway transitions).
7. Student will Let It Go and Move On in conflict situations with peers.
8. Student will apply the problem-solving strategies from the Problem-Solving Chart with peers and adults in structured settings.
9. Student will apply the problem-solving strategies from the Problem-Solving Chart with peers and adults in unstructured settings.

At the very minimum, an observation pretest (see page 27) and posttest should be completed as a basis for tracking progress in independent use of each strategy within the Problem-Solving Chart.

Data Collection Tips

A pretest (see p. 27; see also blank in the Appendix) is completed before introducing the Problem-Solving Chart. The results of this form will yield baseline data against which later observational data can be compared to measure progress. The observer should be somebody who is familiar with the student, such as a parent, teacher, or paraprofessional, and should observe the student in multiple and varied situations that require problem-solving.

Data will be inaccurate if an observer completes the pretest without being familiar with the student in situations that require problem-solving.

Multiple pretests by different observers may be completed to determine if and how a skill is generalizing across environments (e.g., first period to second period, school vs. home, special education classroom vs. general education classroom, unstructured vs. structured environments).

When determining the frequency with which the student uses each problem-solving strategy, only consider the strategies the student chooses independently. Do not include situations where the student was prompted to choose a solution, as this will confuse the data.

Allow time for the student to adequately learn the vocabulary of the Problem-Solving Chart and perform the steps in varied real-life situations. Data can be collected on a daily, weekly, or monthly basis.

The length of time between tests may vary, depending on your need for data collection (e.g., at the end of semester, the end of school year, or when the information is needed prior to a meeting about the student's behavior). If you are keeping data for IEP goals, consider completing a posttest after each nine-week grading period.

Data Collection Sheets

A variety of data sheets may be used. Selection of type of sheet should match IEP objectives and student need.

Problem-Solving Observation – Pretest

Student Name: <u>Karsten</u>   Grade: <u>5th</u>
Person Completing Form: <u>Laure Guyot</u>   Role: <u>Teacher</u>
Directions: Place an "X" in the most appropriate box based on independent use of the strategies.

Date:	Always	Sometimes	Rarely	Never
Seek Help from Adult	X			
Talk It Out and Compromise			X	
Let It Go and Move On			X	
Let It Bother You		X		

Beyond the pretest (later to be repeated as posttest), the following data collection form measures the *effectiveness* of using the Problem-Solving Chart. The outcome is rated using an alphabetical scale (E = excellent, G = good, F = fair, and P = poor), and criteria and should be chosen based on student's behaviors. Effectiveness can be defined in the following manner:

Poor: Student continued to let a problem bother her despite independent or prompted use of Problem-Solving Chart.

Fair: Student went back to the same problem within 5 minutes, despite independent or prompted use of Problem-Solving Chart.

Good: Student re-engaged in general activity within 2 or more minutes with independent or prompted use of Problem-Solving Chart with no evidence of a continued problem.

Excellent: Student re-engaged in general activity within 1 minute or less with independent or prompted use of Problem-Solving Chart with no evidence of a continued problem.

Please note: Letting It Bother You is measured by duration of that behavior rather than intensity. With practice, the amount of time dedicated to the Let it Bother You choice should decrease. An increase in duration over time would signal that the strategy is not working.

This form also provides information on whether the learner demonstrated the skill independently (I) or with a prompt (P).

Problem-Solving: Effectiveness

Student Name: _____ Grade: _____

Person Completing Form: _____ Role: _____

Directions: Indicate (by circling the appropriate letter) for the first three problem-solving steps whether it was completed with a prompt (P) or independently (I).
Then rate each for effectiveness: excellent (E), good (G), fair (F), or poor (P).
Finally, indicate the duration of Let It Bother You if this strategy was used.

Strategy Used	Data Collection by Date					
Date	1/4/13	1/4/13	1/7/13	/ /	/ /	/ /
Location (list)	playground	hallway	playground			
Seek Help From Adult	P I	(P) I	P I	P I	P I	P I
Effectiveness	E G F P	(E) G F P	E G F P	E G F P	E G F P	E G F P
Talk It Out and Compromise	(P) I	P I	P (I)	P I	P I	P I
Effectiveness	E G (F) P	E G F P	E (G) F P	E G F P	E G F P	E G F P
Let It Go and Move On	P (I)	(P) I	P (I)	P I	P I	P I
Effectiveness	E (G) F P	(E) G F P	E (G) F P	E G F P	E G F P	E G F P
Let It Bother You Duration in Minutes	4 min. 15 sec.	2 min.	25 sec.			

(See blank form in the Appendix.) Note: Every strategy will not be used in each situation.

The following data collection sheet can be used to provide a finer analysis of the results of using the Problem-Solving Chart. The data collection sheet is based on the use of total percentages to ensure the student is making progress throughout the process of problem identification, choice of reasonable solution, solution chosen, and resolution of the problem. Even if the student is being prompted through the steps of the chart, progress can be shown in the number of prompts required for each step. For example, if a student is having a hard time choosing a solution, the adult may have to prompt him 10 times by explaining each solution and providing possible outcomes for each. After using the chart for a few days, the student may still need prompting, but the adult may have to explain each option only once. In this example, the reduction in the need for prompts shows improvement and progress.

Problem Identification
Tracked by independent or prompted identification, the student describes the problem situation. The total percentages show the difference between independent identification versus prompted identification of the problem, including the average number of prompts required to identify the problem.

Choice of Reasonable Solution
Tracked by independent or prompted selection, the student selects a strategy from the Problem-Solving Chart. The total percentages show the difference between independent selection vs prompted selection, including the average number of prompts required to choose a reasonable solution.

Solution Chosen
By tracking percentages of which solution the student chooses each time, teachers and parents get a better understanding of the balanced (or unbalanced) use of the solution chosen. Unbalanced use includes choosing only 1-2 of the strategies on the Problem-Solving Chart while omitting other strategies that might be more appropriate.

Resolution of Problem
The effectiveness of the Problem-Solving Chart is measured by the percentages of instances where the problem is actually solved after each use. When a problem is coded as "Yes," the problem was resolved when the student carried out the solution he chose with no additional discourse. When a problem is coded as "No," the problem was unresolved when the student carried out the solution he chose. In this situation, it is likely that the solution chosen was either unsuccessful or the student continued to let the problem bother him.

Let It Bother You
The total number of minutes the student spent choosing the option "Let It Bother You" is also documented on this data collection sheet. This time should decrease as use of the chart becomes more effective. The objective definition for Let It Bother You will be different for each student.

This should be defined at the top of the data collection sheet before data collection begins. For example, one student may get very quiet, withdrawn from a situation and not want to engage in conversation when he is letting a problem bother him, whereas another student may turn red, cry, and yell when he is letting the same problem bother him. Be sure to know the student you are collecting data on well, so you can accurately record the length of time he lets a problem bother him before taking steps to solve the problem.

Progress Monitoring: Total Percentages

Student Name: _____ Grade: _____

Person Completing Form: _____ Role: _____

Student Behaviors for Let It Bother You _____

Date	Description of Problem	Problem Identification Did student identify the problem?	Choice of Reasonable Solution Did student choose a reasonable solution?	Solution Chosen (Circle one)	Was Problem Resolved? (Circle one)	Time Spent Letting It Bother You (Minutes)
		Independent Prompted # of P's _____	Independent Prompted # of P's _____	Let Go Compromise Seek Help	Yes No	
		Independent Prompted # of P's _____	Independent Prompted # of P's _____	Let Go Compromise Seek Help	Yes No	
		Independent Prompted # of P's _____	Independent Prompted # of P's _____	Let Go Compromise Seek Help	Yes No	
		Independent Prompted # of P's _____	Independent Prompted # of P's _____	Let Go Compromise Seek Help	Yes No	
		Independent Prompted # of P's _____	Independent Prompted # of P's _____	Let Go Compromise Seek Help	Yes No	
Totals		Percentage Independent _____ Percentage Prompted _____ Average # of Prompts _____	Percentage Independent _____ Percentage Prompted _____ Average # of Prompts _____	(all Percentages) Let Go ____ Compromise ____ Seek Help ____	Percentage of Problem Resolved Yes _____ Percentage of Problem Unresolved No _____	

Case Study: Wade

The following brief story illustrates data collection with Wade.

Wade, a seventh-grade student, has been in our social skills groups since he was 6 years old. When Wade was in the fourth grade, we started using the problem-solving terminology with him. Wade had problems controlling his anger. He was quick to get upset when he perceived that the rules were unfair. Before we began the process of teaching him problem-solving, we got a baseline to determine his natural skills in the following areas: Seek Help, Talk It Out and Compromise, Let It Go and Move On, and Let It Bother You. As illustrated in his observation pretest, Wade handled most problematic situations by letting things bother him. He often displayed his anger by yelling at others and crying. Many people around him were afraid they might say the wrong thing and upset him.

Problem-Solving Observation – Pretest

Student Name: _____Wade_____ Grade: __4th__

Person Completing Form: ___Jennifer Kirk___ Role: __Teacher__

Directions: Place an "X" in the most appropriate box based on independent choices.

Date: 11/09	Always	Sometimes	Rarely	Never
Seek Help From Adult		X		
Talk It Out and Compromise			X	
Let It Go and Move On				X
Let It Bother You	X			

Comments: Wade currently does not demonstrate that he can let things go, even with prompting. In the school setting, he often lets things bother him for periods ranging from 5 minutes to all day, depending on the incident. If something bothers him, he is rarely able to move past it. Nevertheless, he does Seek Help From Adults on occasion and has been observed to Talk It Out and Compromise. However, Talking It Out is generally initiated by a peer rather than Wade, but he has been observed to share his concerns with a peer without adult prompting. The peer typically leads the compromise that he will follow. On rare occasions, Wade accepts the compromise.

Wade's progress was measured monthly. The following observation form charts his use of the Problem-Solving Chart.

Problem-Solving Observation – Posttest

Student Name: _____Wade_____ Grade: __4th____

Person Completing Form: __Jennifer Kirk____ Role: _Teacher_____

Directions: Place an "x" in the most appropriate box based on independent choices.

Date: 12/9	Always	Sometimes	Rarely	Never
Seek Help From Adult		X		
Talk It Out and Compromise		X		
Let It Go and Move On		X		
Let It Bother You			X	

Comments: As illustrated, Wade has adapted to using the Problem-Solving Chart. He is now quick at independently pursuing a peer to compromise. He occasionally needs prompting to look at the Problem-Solving Chart but does not need additional prompts or assistance besides reminders to look at the chart. He has had a few instances of letting something bother him.

We continued to work with Wade using the terminology from the Problem-Solving Chart. His family integrated the chart into their home, and the terminology was used at school. The posttest was completed at the end of the school year after the Problem-Solving Chart had been in place for six months. As illustrated above, Wade increased his ability to independently Talk It Out and Compromise as well as Let It Go and Move On, and he decreased his behavior of Letting Things Bother Him.

Summary

We have seen that the life skill of problem-solving can be taught through the use of this visual strategy, the Problem-Solving Chart. Because this skill is so critical to success, we have also reviewed approaches to keeping data to monitor progress toward gaining problem-solving skills. The following chapter provides examples of various cases in which this strategy has been utilized. These cases offer further evidence of the effectiveness of this simple strategy.

CHAPTER FOUR

Real-Life Applications of the Problem-Solving Chart

Students with autism spectrum disorders (ASD) are unique in many ways. Although their diagnosis may be the same, every person, every situation is different. The following are true stories from my practice and describe how and why the Problem-Solving Chart was implemented. Notice that we use the specific problem-solving protocol in every situation because it is **(a) visual, (b) concrete, and (c) simple,** and, therefore, is responsive to the unique needs of students with ASD.

The scenarios described in this chapter (Working on a Project With Others, Being Interrupted, Compromising With Peers, Controlling Behavior, Listing Every Wrong and Inclusion Classroom) were chosen to demonstrate how the Problem-Solving Chart is used with different age groups and problem situations through real-world experience.

Working on a Project With Others

"I wish you'd stop telling me to 'Let It Go and Move On.' I'm trying to communicate and work this out." These are words of young professional, Thomas, to his project leader at work. They sat down, ready to work on their project, but Thomas could not get past the fact that he had been motivated to work on this project a month ago when the project leader was not. She was now ready to move forward and get it done. Thomas said his current lack of motivation was due to her failure to work on the project a month earlier.

Was Thomas right to advocate for himself in this situation? It is not our place to judge whether he has the right to continue to bring up past issues over and over, but it cost him his job! Thomas' project leader felt that they spent countless hours talking about things that happened in the past and reported coming to a point where the only choice was to Let Go and Move On in order to be productive.

There are many instances on the job where employees with ASD, like anybody else, are held accountable for moving forward and putting the past behind them. Maturity or chronological age does not equal the ability to Let It Go and Move On. That is, we cannot assume that individuals with ASD will develop the skill of Letting Go and Moving On without direct instruction.

Unfortunately, Thomas had not been directly taught this skill by the time he was 20. He is starting to learn it now; however, the process typically takes longer for adults to learn as they are developing new habits and must "undo" the way they have processed information for years.

Getting Interrupted

Joseph, a sixth grader, was very disturbed when someone interrupted him while he was talking at drama camp. For three hours (until it was time to leave for the day), he continued to bring it up in front of the student who had interrupted him. Our staff introduced the Problem-Solving Chart to Joseph as soon as we saw his inability to move forward. We wanted drama camp to be a positive experience for him but knew he would not get the maximum benefit of his time with peers unless he could put his grievances aside. As the day went on, Joseph was not "connecting" with the chart, but we continued to use it. We went through the strategies, one by one. He told us that he was Letting It Go and Moving On, but he clearly was not. We reminded him, "If you are still talking about the problem, then you have not moved on."

When Joseph's mother picked him up that afternoon, we gave her a copy of the Problem-Solving Chart so that she could practice with Joseph. For this strategy to work, it was important to use the same terminology in the community and at home. In the past, Joseph's mom had felt that she did not have the tools to handle her son's hyper-focusing on a topic and often reverted to "Oh, Joseph ..." She was willing to give our new terminology a try.

After two days of repetition of "Let It Go," Joseph was able to let the issue go. We applied the chart to other situations to make sure he generalized the skill. We used the same visual chart with him for over a year, because learning to apply the skill effectively and independently was critical. After a few months, he told us to just Let It Go and Move On rather than debriefing with him about the problem. At that point, we knew he was close to "getting it."

Be patient when using this strategy. You are retraining someone's way of thinking and must allow time for a mental shift. This skill does not come naturally for many, and certainly not for individuals with ASD.

Compromising With Peers

Hudson, a second grader, participates in a weekly social skills group. During social group, students of this age are taught to plan and initiate their own games, rather than having games determined in advance by staff. We have found that this helps students with initiation, decision-making, teamwork, and problem-solving.

When Hudson first started in the group, he would enter the room with a grandiose idea of what he wanted to play that day. He was certain his peers would want to play the same game as he did. If the other kids said "no," Hudson felt he had not explained himself well enough, so he attempted to re-explain his idea.

One day, when Hudson received the answer of "no" – friends did not want to play his game – we reminded him that sometimes you can compromise by using the First-Then Rule: First ___ (*their idea*) Then ____ (*another's idea*). Using this rule allows everyone to play at least one thing that they want to play (see the Three Rules of Compromise on p. 21). He was overwhelmed with that idea. He thought that it was too much work – compromising is often difficult, especially for individuals with ASD. I could tell that Hudson was getting stressed, so I asked him to step into the hallway with me in hopes of allowing him a break from the situation and an opportunity to refocus.

As soon as we stepped into the hallway, Hudson burst into tears. He thought that rock-paper-scissors should be part of compromising because it was easier than working out a compromise. I said that would be fine; we could make a list for him that consisted of four compromising strategies with rock-paper-scissors being the first choice. At that point, he had won – I had accepted his idea. However, it wasn't over. Hudson wanted to write in pen on the chart. I would not allow him to write rock-paper-scissors on the chart because it did not apply to everyone else in the group. (Our group rules concerning compromise are based on strategies that are appropriate for use through adulthood without looking childish.) Instead, I got out a sheet of paper, and we made his rules of compromise, which included rock-paper-scissors. Hudson still could not move on. At that moment, I knew that we would have to use the Problem-Solving Chart as a supplement to the Three Rules of Compromise.

Once we were using both charts, the Three Rules of Compromise and the Problem-Solving Chart, things started to go a little easier. It still took a few months of applying the Problem-Solving Chart and the modified Rules of Compromise during numerous naturally occurring play dates before Hudson was able to carry out the skills independently.

Controlling Behavior

Sam, an 11th-grade student, has meltdowns at school that require him to be sent home early on some days. He complains about his aide and often feels provoked and pushed to his limit. As a consultant with his school, I observed the meltdowns.

Teachers referred to this student as manipulative and felt that he was using his behavior to get out of work. For example, one day he did not want to do any more writing because he felt that what he had written for the assignment was enough. Once he was done, he was done! He could not think of any more sentences, even though he had written less than the half page assigned. His aide encouraged him to write a few more sentences. The aide's strategy was appropriate, but it was not well received. At that point, instead of backing off, the aide continued talking to Sam. The special education teacher approached to intervene, stating, "It's your grade, and we are not going to argue with you about it to get it done."

As I watched all of this transpire, all I could think was "Talk It Out and Compromise." I didn't mean that Sam should talk it out with the special education teacher; he needed to go to the source – the teacher who gave this assignment.

I introduced the Problem-Solving Chart to Sam. He comprehended the material quickly and decided to attempt to Talk It Out and Compromise with the teacher who had assigned the paper. It worked! The teacher decided that he had written enough for a good grade. Together, Sam and I looked at the Problem-Solving Chart again to debrief what he had done that had yielded effective results with minimal conflict. We talked about whether or not this was something that he would be able to use in order to prevent shutting down in other environments. Something appeared to be missing as an option for him. To clear his head, sometimes he needed a 5-minute break. We added the 5-minute break to his chart (see p. 38).

It is still unclear whether the Problem-Solving Chart will work for Sam to decrease his meltdowns and increase his ability to problem solve effectively and independently. His school staff is not convinced that he needs a visual support like this because they have known him for a long time and have not seen changes in his behavior since he was in middle school. No matter how many specialists come in, the staff will have to follow through every day and with every problem in order for Sam to memorize and apply the strategies independently.

Individuals with ASD need a concrete framework to use for problem-solving – something simple that can be applied to any problem situation. It may seem too simple to work. But that is the exact reason it often works – because it is simple and easy to remember in the moment of frustration. During Sam's meltdowns and resolution before being introduced to the Problem-Solving Chart, he always focused on the problem itself and was unable to make the mental shift to another option for working it out. If the chart is used consistently, Sam will be able to focus on the strategies for solving problems and come to a resolution.

Sam's Problem-Solving Chart

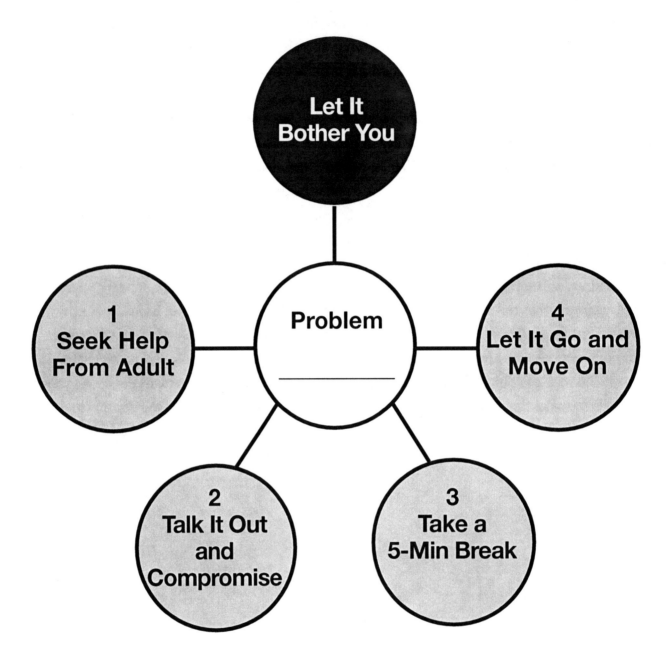

Listing Every Wrong

Brandon is in the fourth grade. He is very intelligent and is included in the general education classroom. His current special interests include courtrooms, dressing up in suits, and amputations. Brandon functions well at school with a few reported issues in PE. At social group, we see a delay in processing of events that often results in him bringing up his concerns after a given situation has ended. He remembers things from the first social group months ago, specifically anything that anyone did wrong, often spouting lists of every wrong anybody has ever done. When he has a problem, he often yells "You're not listening to me" or "You don't care about me."

I introduced the Problem-Solving Chart as a means to help Brandon to learn to let go of his grievances toward others. I changed the color of the positive strategies from green to red because red was his favorite color (see comment about colors on p. 5). I also changed the wording from "Let It Go and Move On" to "Dismiss" because of his interest in and understanding of courtrooms and legal terminology.

Brandon has been using the Problem-Solving Chart for three months both at social group and at home. He still uses the chart to help him to know when to use the various strategies, but now can quickly dismiss with one verbal prompt. He is using Talk It Out and Compromise independently at least once in each social group. He is given verbal praise when use of the appropriate problem-solving strategies is observed. Although he is quick to "dismiss" in a social group setting with peers, he has to continue using the chart to help him become more independent with it and generalize use of the chart to every problem situation in other settings.

Brandon's Problem-Solving Chart

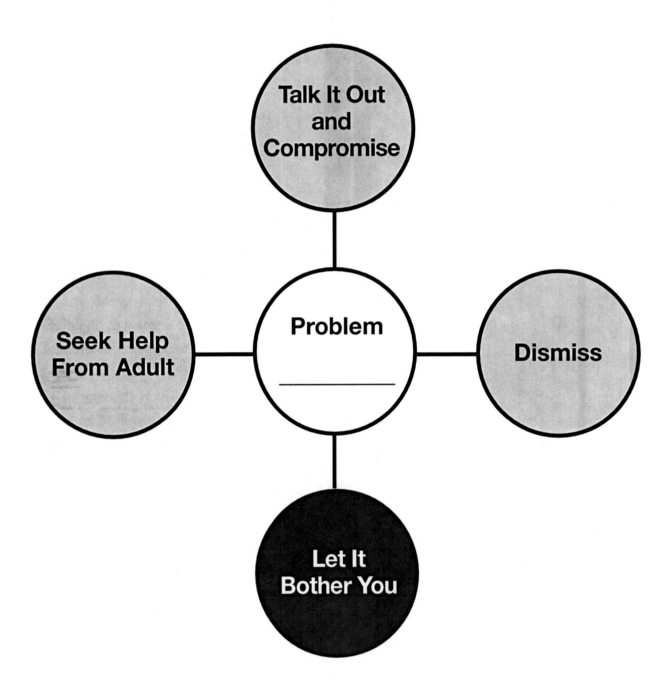

Inclusion Classroom

Blake, a first-grade student in an inclusion classroom, was very interested in interacting with his peers and initiated many such interactions, but he often got into arguments related to turn-taking, winning/losing, not being chosen as a partner, or not playing a game correctly. Blake also struggled academically and became very frustrated and agitated when subjects and assignments were difficult for him.

When problems with peers arose, he sometimes accepted majority rule about what to play, but at other times he continued to argue for his own idea. In short, he lacked consistent problem-solving skills.

His teacher began using the Problem-Solving Chart. She enlarged a copy and put it on a wall in the classroom (the whole class was also taught the basics of the chart). Within a few days, Blake began to identify the problem independently and to choose a strategy. After two months, he could use the chart fluently with the assistance of an adult; however, if an adult simply sent him to the chart, Blake had trouble choosing a solution.

Despite his successes, Blake's teacher was becoming frustrated that he was not moving more quickly towards independent use of his problem-solving skills. After much discussion with other teachers, it was determined that perhaps Blake was not comfortable with reading the words independently. Since he had proven himself to be a visual learner in the classroom, his teacher decided to add symbols to each strategy on the chart. Within one day, Blake was successfully using the chart independently. This small variation of the chart gave Blake the confidence to solve problems independently and to use the chart successfully on his own.

Blake's Problem-Solving Chart

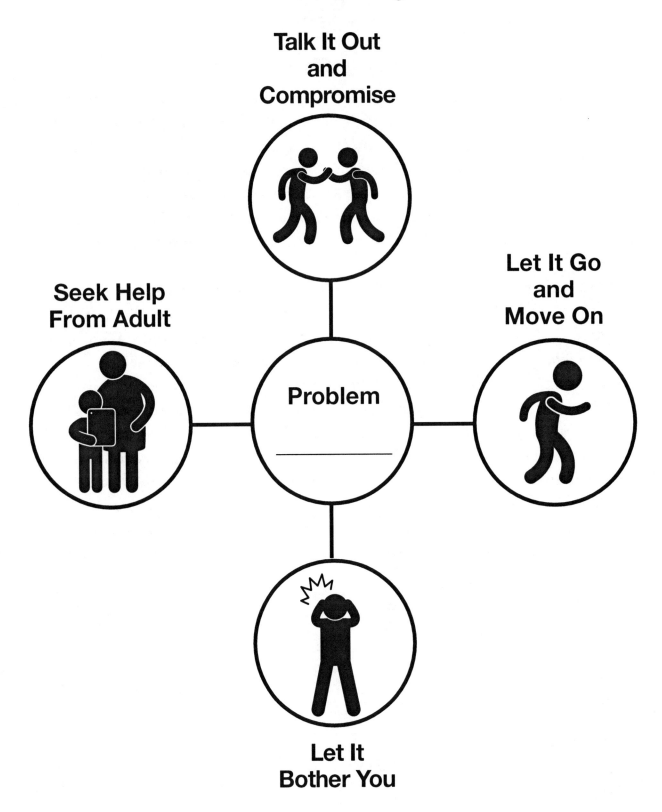

Summary

I hope the examples in this chapter will help readers to apply the Problem-Solving Chart with their own students. Each situation is from a different setting and is unique in the way the implementer and the student responded to the chart and the accompanying strategies. The examples also demonstrate the use of variations to accommodate individual needs, including adding visuals to each choice, changing colors, wording, font size, and type, or inserting an additional choice (i.e., a break).

Following are Frequently Asked Questions. My intent was to make the Frequently Asked Questions section a place where students with high-functioning ASD can go and read for themselves. If for some reason it is not a good option for a student with ASD to read on his own, teachers and other adults may want to paraphrase or otherwise work through the situations with him.

Frequently Asked Questions

Seek Help

Question: I have asked for help before, and it did not work. The adult I asked would not help me. What should I do?

Answer: Most adults want to give their students and children the power to work out situations on their own, so they might direct you to "work it out." If you do not feel comfortable with your ability to work it out, ask for specific help. Consider sharing the Problem-Solving Chart with an adult who knows you well. This will help the person understand the skills you want to learn and support you in gaining them.

Question: Kids call me a "tattle tale" when I seek help from an adult. What should I do differently?

Answer: Make sure you are not using "seek help" to solve every problem. Sometimes your problem might be that you feel uncomfortable. Everyone feels uncomfortable at times, but that does not *always* mean that they need help. Make sure you have a legitimate problem rather than telling on others who have a problem. You have to allow others to work out their problems on their own. They might choose not to involve an adult but work it out with each other instead, or they might choose to just let it go. That is their choice. Try not to get involved in problems if they do not involve you. Exceptions would be if someone is hurt or being bullied. In those situations, it still might be best to pursue help from an adult in private, where your peers do not see that you are telling on them.

Talk It Out and Compromise

Question: I try to talk it out, but I am not good at coming up with a compromise. What should I do?

Answer: Make sure you are doing the following steps when talking it out:

1. **Use a neutral tone.** Using a harsh or negative tone will make the other person defensive. The other person's response will be different if he or she feels attacked rather than understood.

2. **Listen without interrupting.** Interrupting can be interpreted negatively. It also breaks up the flow of the conversation. If you interrupt too frequently, the other person might shut down and not want to talk further. If you get interrupted, politely ask, "May I finish?" in a neutral tone. If you get upset about being interrupted, the problem has switched from what was being discussed to your frustration about being interrupted, so think of a way to calmly restate what it is that you wish to communicate and be ready to listen to another's response.

3. **Guide the conversation toward a compromise.** Talking it out is only one part of the solution. If the talking does not lead to a compromise, the step is incomplete. Without a compromise, there is no closure. Also, this leaves your relationship open to the same problem coming up again. Use scripts that will help you move toward a compromise (e.g., "Where do we go from here?" "How can we move forward?" "How can we compromise?" "Is there anything I can do to compromise and make this better?").

4. **Try to use "I" statements.** "I" statements share your concerns from your perspective whereas "you" statements often sound accusatory or blaming. People are less likely to work toward a compromise if they feel accused of or blamed for something ("**I** feel like you were not listening to me" vs. "**You** were not listening to me").

5. **Allow for cool down.** Make sure that both you and others involved are in a state of mind conducive to talking and compromise. If you are upset, please refer to the strategies on pages 12-13 to assist you in calming down. Give the other person time to cool down as well. If the other person involved is someone who cannot talk using a calm tone, talking it out and compromising may not be an option.

Question: No one listens to me. They don't care about my feelings. What should I do?

Answer: It sounds like you are trying to talk it out, but it depends on how you are doing it. This is a complicated situation that may require intervention from someone who is more familiar with your situation. Feeling unheard or not understood can be a signal of depression or low self-esteem. Another explanation could be that you are not effectively communicating your thoughts to others. Finally, make sure you are listening carefully to others. It goes both ways. In trying to come up with a strategy consider the following.

1. What is your true intention behind what you are trying to communicate? Are you trying to be helpful or hurtful? If you are feeling jealous or angry, chances are that your communication comes across as hurtful. Avoid using a rude, negative, or condescending tone.

2. Are you using generalizations, including the terms *always* and *never*? Using such terms weakens your ability to communicate because they are not accurate. It is rare that someone *always* or *never* does something. Avoid using phrases like these as that would make the other person feel defensive. If it is true, you can say, "I have heard you say that before," instead of saying, "You always say that," which is an exaggeration of the truth.

3. When are you trying to talk? Timing is extremely important. You can be saying the right things but at the wrong time. Consider the timing and choose wisely. If you would like to share with a friend something that is very exciting to you, it is not the right time to do so if he is sad, mad, or even very excited about something else. Wait for a calm moment when your friend may be able to listen carefully and focus on you. Make sure there are no distractions.

4. Be cautious using this terminology ("No one ever listens to me") because it can come across as complaining. People typically show little tolerance for somebody complaining and the "Woe Is Me" Syndrome, as it generally signals that you are feeling sorry for yourself rather than being willing to do something about it. This can further push away others and make you feel even more alone and less heard.

5. Consider the difference between people *listening to* you and people *agreeing with* you. Do you want someone to listen and acknowledge what you have said or just agree with you? Basically, what are your expectations? There are situations where someone will listen without agreeing. This is okay, because people have different opinions.

Let It Go and Move On

Question: I have been told I have monomania – that is, I am often confined to one thought. I know I pick out one detail and hyper-focus on it. What can I do to let it go and move on?

Answer: You have to find a strategy that works for you. After surveying individuals with ASD who struggled with monomania, we found that the following were their top strategies.

Strategies for Letting It Go

1. Start a journal – Write down your thoughts; it does not have to be in any particular format. You can write bullet points, lists, sentences, paragraphs, letters, etc. An example format might be "I feel ____ because ____. I will ____." Write your thoughts down in a journal to help you visualize your actions over a period of time. By writing down your thoughts, you can see trends in specific situations that lead to negative emotions with long-term effects/consequences of your anger. Writing down personal thoughts may help you process what you are feeling to allow you to eventually let it go.
2. Write a note or draft an email (but do not send it). If you are upset with someone, it can be helpful to write a pretend letter or email without sending it. This will allow you to vent your feelings. Typing your thoughts can be a great way "to get something off your chest" without making the other person uncomfortable or upset. Be sure to destroy the written words so no one is able to later find them.
3. Change the company you keep. People you are around may be constant reminders of the very thing you are trying to move on from. If there is a group of people who are boisterous, and it is easy for you to get agitated, look for a quieter person or group that may help you to feel more peaceful. Sometimes hanging out with the old group can lead you to fall back into the very behaviors and thought patterns you are trying to change.
4. Change your scenery. Your environment has a greater effect on you than you realize. The environment you are in can add to you being happy, sad, depressed, or angry.

Some environments are a constant reminder of the problem you are facing. If you are upset, try going some place that makes you feel good as a means to help "let go" of any anger. You may need to change your scenery for a moment or indefinitely. Be cautious not to always escape your problems. If you find you are constantly changing your scenery, there may be additional issues with escape or avoidance that need to be addressed.

5. Stay busy with something else. Staying busy with something else is essentially a "cool-down" for anger. Cooling down allows you to let things go more quickly. Usually, expressing the initial anger causes more harm than good. By distracting yourself and staying busy, you may overcome the initial anger or uncontrollable feeling.

6. Use a silly word or phrase, such as "Laughter is the best medicine." By lightening your mood, you may realize that the issue is not that big of a deal and you can let it go more quickly. You may want to use scripting to define a word or phrase you can always say to pull you out of a heavy mood.

7. Think of something positive in your life. Anger can cloud your judgment. By thinking of something positive, you may realize how insignificant the problem really is.

8. Agree to disagree. To be able to let something go without a compromise can be difficult. Agreeing to disagree is saying that both you and the other person agree that you will disagree on the subject matter, but you are both okay with that. It shows that both parties have expressed their views. Although compromise was not reached officially, both parties are wiling to let it go.

9. Know you have tried the other options and need to move forward. Sometimes you will find that you have tried other options with no resolution. Rather than focusing on the negative, let things go and move forward. This can be easier said than done; however, it is necessary to move forward without continuing unhealthy feelings of anger and resentment.

10. Live in the present rather than the past. Some people linger in resentment over things and are likely to hold a grudge toward others. This is never a positive solution. Live in the present and focus on what is going on today.

Question: In elementary school, I did not like it when someone told me to "let it go and move on." I felt like that was easy for them to say. It was extremely frustrating because I felt like I was being told it was not okay to have feelings. What should I do?

Answer: Telling someone to "let it go and move on" can be interpreted negatively. No one wants to be told what to do. Everyone has feelings. Your feelings are very important. If someone asks you to "let it go and move on," it is usually for one of the following reasons:

1. They see that you are stressed about something you cannot change.
2. They feel they have heard your concerns and you are repeating yourself.
3. They feel badly about what happened and want to change it, but they need you to move on to see that they can change.
4. They are ready to change topics.
5. The conversation on the topic has ended.
6. They do not want to discuss it anymore (at that time or ever).

Because many individuals with ASD have tunnel vision (difficulty taking the perspective of others, often called mindblindness), it is easy for them to focus on details too long without realizing or considering what the listener is thinking. People give you clues that they are ready to be done with conversation. They might say "all righty then," or "Okay, we will talk about that later." Have people tell you what they generally say when they are ready to move on. Even if they are not always conscious of it, everyone has a script they use that can be a signal to someone else.

REFERENCES

Abendroth, K., & Damico, J. (2009). Catastrophic reactions of a child with an autism spectrum disorder: A social phenomenon. *Asia Pacific Journal of Speech, Language, and Hearing, 12*, 263-273.

Bellini, S., & Peters, J. K. (2008). Social skills training for youth with autism spectrum disorders. *Child and Adolescent Psychiatric Clinics of North America, 17*, 857-873.

Buron, K. D., & Curtis, M. B. (2012). *The incredible 5-point scale: The significantly improved and expanded second edition – Assisting students in understanding social interactions and controlling their emotional responses*. Shawnee Mission, KS: AAPC Publishing.

Centers for Medicare and Medicaid Services. (2009). *Autism spectrum disorders: Final report on environmental scan*. Washington, DC: Author.

Collucci, A. (2011). *Big picture thinking – Using central coherence theory to support social skills*. Shawnee Mission, KS: AAPC Publishing.

Crane, L., Pring, L., Ryder, N., & Hermelin, B. (2011). Executive functions in savant artists with autism. *Research in Autism Spectrum Disorders, 5*, 790-797.

Deitchman, C., Reeve, S., Reeve, K. F., & Progar, P. R. (2010). Incorporating video feedback into self-management training to promote generalization of social initiation by children with autism. *Education and Treatment of Children, 33*, 475-488.

Frith, U. (2004). Emanuel Miller lecture: Confusions and controversies about Asperger Syndrome. *Journal of Child Psychology and Psychiatry, 45*(4), 672-686.

Geurts, H. M., Verté, S., Oosterlaan, J., Roéyers, H., & Sergeant, J. A. (2004). How specific are executive functioning deficits in attention deficit hyperactivity disorder and autism? *Journal of Child Psychology and Psychiatry, 45*(4), 836-1254.

Grandin, T. (2009). How does visual thinking work in the mind of a person with autism? A personal account. *Philosophical Transactions of the Royal Society, 364*, 1437-1442. doi: 10.1098/rstb.2008.0297

Hill, E. L. (2004). Executive dysfunction in autism. *Trends in Cognitive Sciences, 8*(1), 26-32.

Hill, E. L., & Bird, C. M. (2006). Executive processes in Asperger Syndrome: Patterns of performance in multiple case series. *Neuropsychologia, 44*(14), 2822-2835.

Kaland, N., Mortensen, E. L., & Smith, L. (2011). Social communication impairments in children and adolescents with Asperger Syndrome: Slow response time and the impact of prompting. *Research in Autism Spectrum Disorders*, 1129-1137.

Kim, J. A., Szatmari, P., Bryson, S. E., Streiner, D. L., & Wilson, F. J. (2000). The prevalence of anxiety and mood problems among children with autism and Asperger syndrome. *Autism, 4*(2), 117-132.

Lofland, K. (2010). *Getting the teacher's attention.* Unpublished manuscript. Bloomington, IN: Indiana Resource Center on Autism.

Minshew, N. J., Meyer, J., & Goldstein, G. (2002). Abstract reasoning in autism: dissociation between concept formation and concept identification. *Neuropsychology, 16,* 327-334.

Moore, S. T. (2002). *Asperger Syndrome and the elementary school experience.* Shawnee Mission, KS: AAPC Publishing.

Myles, B. S., & Southwick, J. (2005). *Asperger Syndrome and difficult moments: Practical solutions for tantrums, rage, and meltdowns (2nd ed.).* Shawnee Mission, KS: AAPC Publishing.

National Autism Center. (2009). *National standards report: Addressing the need for evidence-based practice guidelines for autism spectrum disorders.* Randolph, MA: Author.

National Professional Development Center on Autism Spectrum Disorders. (n.d). *Evidence-based practice briefs.* Retrieved from http://autismpdc.fpg.unc.edu/content/briefs.

Nefdt, N., Koegel, R., Singer, G., & Gerber, M. (2009). The use of a self-directed learning program to provide introductory training in pivotal response treatment to parents of children with autism. *The Journal of Positive Behavior Interventions, 12*(1), 23-32.

Ostryn, C., & Wolfe, P. (2011). Teaching children with autism to ask "what's that?" using picture communication with vocal results. *Infants and Young Children, 24,* 174-192.

Ritvo, R. A., Ritvo, E. R., Guthrie, D., Yuwlier, A., Ritvo, M. J., & Weisbender, L. (2008). A scale to assist the diagnosis of autism and Asperger's disorder in adults (RAADS): A pilot of study. *Journal of Autism and Developmental Disorders, 38,* 213-223.

Vismara, L. A., & Rogers, S. J. (2010). Behavior treatments in autism spectrum disorder: What do we know? *Annual Review of Clinical Psychology, 6,* 446-468.

Wichnick, A. M., Vener, S. M., Pyrtek, M., & Poulson, C. L. (2010). The effect of a scriptfading procedure on responses to peer initiations among young children with autism. *Research in Autism Spectrum Disorders, 4,* 290-299.

Reproducible Forms

- Problem-Solving Chart
- Observation Pretest
- Observation Posttest
- Problem-Solving: Effectiveness
- Problem-Solving: Selection, Demonstration, Independence, and Effectiveness
- 5-Point Scale

Problem-Solving Chart

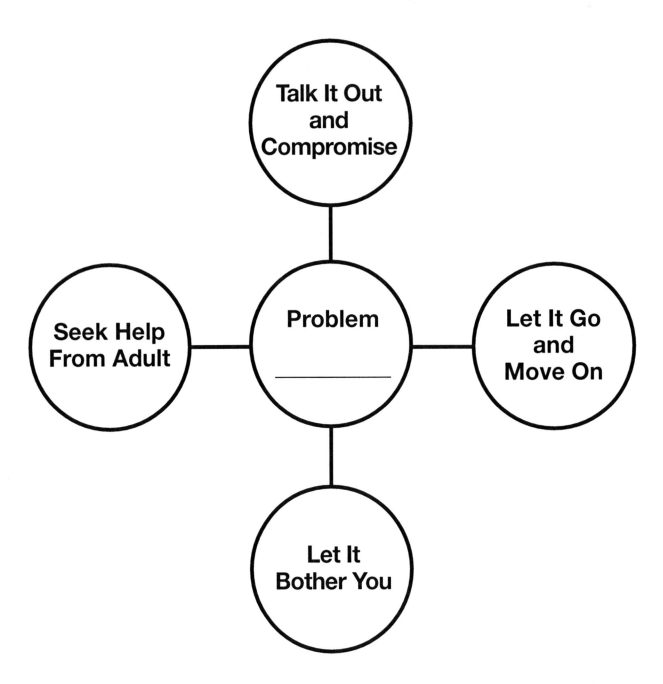

Problem-Solving Observation – Pretest

Student Name: _____ Grade: _____

Person Completing Form:_____

Role: _____

Directions: Place an "X" in the most appropriate box based on independent use of the strategies.

Date:	Always	Sometimes	Rarely	Never
Seek Help from Adult				
Talk It Out and Compromise				
Let It Go and Move On				
Let It Bother You				

Comments: _____

_____

_____

_____

_____

_____

_____

Problem-Solving Observation – Posttest

Student Name: _____ Grade: _____

Person Completing Form:_____

Role: _____

Directions: Place an "X" in the most appropriate box based on independent use of the strategies.

Date:	Always	Sometimes	Rarely	Never
Seek Help from Adult				
Talk It Out and Compromise				
Let It Go and Move On				
Let It Bother You				

Comments: _____

_____

_____

_____

_____

_____

_____

Problem-Solving: Effectiveness

Student Name: _____ Grade: _____

Person Completing Form:_____

Role: _____

Directions: Indicate (by circling the appropriate letter) for the first three problem-solving steps whether it was completed with a prompt (P) or independently (I).

Then rate each for effectiveness: excellent (E), good (G), fair (F), or poor (P).

E _____

G _____

F _____

P _____

Finally, indicate the duration of Let It Bother You if this strategy was used.

Strategy Used	Data Collection by Date					
Date	/ /	/ /	/ /	/ /	/ /	/ /
Location (list)						
Seek Help From Adult	P I	P I	P I	P I	P I	P I
Effectiveness	E G F P	E G F P	F G F P	E G F P	E G F P	E G F P
Talk It Out and Compromise	P I	P I	P I	P I	P I	P I
Effectiveness	E G F P	E G F P	E G F P	E G F P	E G F P	E G F P
Let It Go and Move On	P I	P I	P I	P I	P I	P I
Effectiveness	E G F P	E G F P	E G F P	E G F P	E G F P	E G F P
Let It Bother You Duration in Minutes						

Progress Monitoring: Total Percentages

Student Name: _____ Grade: _____

Person Completing Form:_____

Role: _____

Student Behaviors for Let It Bother You _____

Date	Description of Problem	Problem Identification Did student identify the problem?	Choice of Reasonable Solution Did student choose a reasonable solution?	Solution Chosen (Circle one)	Was Problem Resolved? (Circle one)	Time Spent Letting It Bother You (Minutes)
		Independent Prompted # of P's _____	Independent Prompted # of P's _____	Let Go Compromise Seek Help	Yes No	
		Independent Prompted # of P's _____	Independent Prompted # of P's _____	Let Go Compromise Seek Help	Yes No	
		Independent Prompted # of P's _____	Independent Prompted # of P's _____	Let Go Compromise Seek Help	Yes No	
		Independent Prompted # of P's _____	Independent Prompted # of P's _____	Let Go Compromise Seek Help	Yes No	
		Independent Prompted # of P's _____	Independent Prompted # of P's _____	Let Go Compromise Seek Help	Yes No	
Totals		Percentage Independent _____ Percentage Prompted _____ Average # of Prompts _____	Percentage Independent _____ Percentage Prompted _____ Average # of Prompts _____	(all Percentages) Let Go ____ Compromise ____ Seek Help ____	Percentage of Problem Resolved Yes _____ Percentage of Problem Unresolved No _____	

5-Point Scale

Name: _____ My _____ Scale

Rating	Looks like	Feels like	I can *try* to
5			
4			
3			
2			
1			

PUBLISHING

... *Your First Source for Practical Solutions for Autism Spectrum and Related Disorders*

**For these and all other
AAPC books and materials,
got to www.aapcpubishing.net**

P.O. Box 23173
Shawnee Mission, Kansas 66283-0173
www.aapcpublishing.net

CPSIA information can be obtained at www.ICGtesting.com
Printed in the USA
BVOW051211120213

313045BV00008B/183/P